Being a Christian in a Corrupt World:

A Continual Fight for Justice

By La'Asia Cesar

La'Asia Cesar

Being a Christian in a Corrupt World:

A Continual Fight for Justice

Acknowledgments

In my memoir, I want to express profound gratitude for the unwavering love of God, which has been my guiding light through the darkest storms and the calmest seas. Despite facing excommunication and isolation from the communities, families, and governments that once surrounded me, I found solace and peace within myself, knowing that God's love never wavers. I am eternally thankful for all that He has done for me, shielding me with His love during times of need and enveloping me with His peace in every circumstance.

Dedications

To my beloved daughters, Le'Onna and Gi'Asia,

As I embark on sharing my journey, I want to express my deep love for both of you. My fervent prayer is that amidst life's trials, God grants you enduring peace. Remember, even in the face of rejection, His unwavering presence will guide you through every storm.

Happy Birthday Le'Onna and Congratulations Gi'Asia! May you both continue to shine brightly. With love, your devoted mother.

With all my love,
La'Asia Cesar

Introduction

In the pages that follow, I invite you on a journey through the passages of justice, where shattered hopes and defeated dreams tested my faith in the system – a journey that I hope will serve as a guide to inspire those who have battled with the disappointment of deceptive justice.

Readers will discover the profound influence of divine intervention within the justice system. As we remain steadfast in our authenticity and uphold our testimonies aligned with the divine, the boundless possibilities with God by our side will become evident.

My faith journey has significantly shaped who I am today, particularly through experiencing God's blessings when I've felt overwhelmed by societal challenges and the justice system.

Navigating challenges in one's faith journey can be deeply personal and complex. For me, grappling with the division of individuals claiming to adhere to Christian principles while resorting to coercive measures, like excommunication and government corruption, has been particularly difficult. It's disheartening when those who profess faith fail to uphold its core beliefs of love, justice, and compassion. Standing up to injustice amid such adversity requires immense strength and resilience, and I have been left alone with courage in navigating these trials.

For me, faith intertwined with prayer is paramount—it sets the tone in my household and acts as the glue binding my family together. Despite having a dominant personality, it's through faith in my God that I find the calm amidst life's storms. In a community where access to resources are limited when fighting against injustice, I primarily rely on my faith to navigate challenges."

My family has been instrumental in guiding my spiritual journey. At around 20 years old, I encountered a poignant story of a woman who tragically lost her life while helping others. This incident deeply resonated with me, stirring a profound sense of empathy and vulnerability as a parent. It compelled me to seek comfort and security through faith in God, as a means to alleviate the sorrow and fear for both the victim and my own loved ones."

Through my spiritual experiences, I've learned that not everyone is genuine. There are many deceitful individuals in our midst who prioritize personal gain over justice and assistance. This phenomenon, often termed 'kissing buts', highlights the prevalence of insincerity. Despite this, I remain steadfast in my commitment to stand up for what is right.

My hope is that this memoir will inspire readers to recognize that faith in God can sustain those who have been ostracized from communities and denied justice. In a world where human judgment often fails, it's crucial to remember that ultimate authority lies with God. Holding onto our faith in Him can render all other judgments irrelevant, as His divine will ultimately prevail.

My memoir will explore the theme of triumph over adversity, where I've experienced divine intervention overcoming injustices within the legal system. It will also touch on the importance of faith and divine guidance during dark times, showcasing how belief in God can bring hope and miracles even in the most challenging situations. Additionally, it will highlight personal transformation and renewal through my ongoing spiritual journey, despite encountering individuals who claim Christian values yet act in ways contrary to them.

Not many people talk about being ostracized from a government community due to speaking out against police brutality and governmental injustice while being deemed a Christian. I am that person within this situation. I have experienced many government interceptions and still live in this community. I believe that this is God's job to be done in this community. There are many more people that have experienced this, but may not have had the chance to voice it. I thank God for giving me the opportunity to do so.

Chapter 1

Confronting a Legal Notice

Upon opening the door, I was met with the stern visage of a Sheriff, his presence both unexpected and disconcerting. He wasted no time in delivering his message—I had been served. My initial instinct was to reach for my phone, hoping to document the encounter on Facebook Live. However, my efforts were in vain; only a fragment of the interaction was captured, the center of the matter lost to the digital realm.

Reluctantly, I turned my attention back to the Sheriff, who presented me with a document to sign. It was then that the gravity of the situation dawned on me—I had been served with a "Failure to Send" notice, citing Maryland Education Code Section 7-301. My mind raced with questions, the implications of this legal notice weighing heavily on my thoughts.

As I recall that serene, cold, sun-drenched morning, it feels as vivid as if it were just yesterday. In the town of Princess Anne, sunlight streamed gently through the windows, casting warm patches on the floor where my little one lay snug beneath her blankets. Outside, the usual bustle of traffic was notably absent, a rare reprieve from the daily rush of local school and work commuters in our bustling community of government officials and business owners. With my 17-year-old off at school and my husband out running errands, the solitude was palpable, heightening my awareness of every sound and movement. As I hesitated before answering the door, I couldn't help but wonder who might be on the other side.

It's not new that I, the protagonist, along with my family, have all felt the impact of harassment from members of our community, as well as officials from the local government who either failed to address the issue or were complicit in it.

But to see a Sheriff at the door without a call made by myself about their or the community harassment was nonexistent until this turning point.

I was the one that always filed court documents against them.

And now the tables have turned.

I vividly recount moments where I felt guided by divine intervention through legal injustices, shining a light on the profound role of faith during times of darkness. Within my family congregation, I faced rejection and prejudice that mirrored the injustices I encountered elsewhere. The pastor, with military ties, employed tactics akin to those of the wider community. Seeking solace, my family turned to another church, only to find ourselves uncomfortably close to law enforcement—a stark reminder of the challenges within the Tri County Communities of Maryland. These experiences forced me to confront the dissonance between professed Christian values and their real-world application, laying the foundation for my ongoing journey of spiritual transformation and resilience.

I felt the weight of destiny pressing upon me, urging a profound shift in my life's course. The summoning by the Somerset County Circuit Courts marked not just a legal challenge, but a spiritual trial, testing the strength of my faith in God. Bewildered and uncertain, I battled with the deeper significance of this unforeseen turn of events. It was a moment demanding clarity and introspection, especially as I had recently made the decision to enroll my child in a private homeschooling program—a choice fraught with its own implications. This confluence of events propelled me into a journey of seeking deeper understanding and meaning, poised on the brink of transformation.

In that moment, I sensed the hand of God guiding me through the chaos. Despite facing what seemed like orchestrated challenges from the Somerset County Board of Education, I found solace in my faith. With no means to hire legal representation, I resolved to stand for myself in the face of adversity. Amidst the legal proceedings of case C19JV23000057, I clung to my belief that God's grace would prevail over the forces arrayed against me.

 Reflecting on your experiences, have you ever encountered challenges or persecution from your community or local government? How did you navigate those situations, and in what ways did your faith influence your response? If you haven't faced such challenges, consider how you might respond if you were to encounter them.

Now that these questions have been proposed amongst us. I began to reflect on my future court battle. As I reflected on the looming battle with the Somerset County Board of Education, I began to feel a stirring within me—an assurance that despite the trials ahead, I wasn't alone. With each obstacle that arose, I turned inward, drawing strength from my faith, knowing that even without legal representation, I would stand firm. Little did I know then, amidst the unfolding legal proceedings of case C19JV23000057, this unwavering belief in God's guidance would become my greatest source of resilience against the forces aligned against me.

Nothing means more to parents than striving to safeguard their child's well-being, especially in the realm of education. Despite my efforts, my community's hostility towards my family persisted. Each attempt to protect my child, whether through public schooling, homeschooling under official supervision, or enrolling her in a private school, was met with adversity. The bruises she came home with from public school haunted me, as staff members either mocked, gaslit, or ignored my concerns. Even under the oversight of Somerset County Board of Education, the same patterns of mistreatment persisted. When I finally sought refuge in a private school, I was met with legal challenges. My frustration and desperation led me to turn to a higher power for intervention. Gathering evidence of my daughter's schooling, I filed a motion with the courts, feeling the weight of unnecessary obstacles placed in my path. Despite my repeated attempts to communicate with the school system, my efforts were consistently disregarded. It was a deeply isolating and unjust experience, one where I felt my only recourse was to fight for my child's right to a safe and nurturing educational environment.

In the midst of navigating the trials posed by a corrupt government and dwelling among its officials within my community, a Somerset County District Court Bailiff once asserted, 'you have no rights,' leaving me to grapple for my freedoms. Yet, amidst daunting odds, I find ease in the cards dealt by God, as I embark on the relentless battle to safeguard my rights. The fierce determination of a parent to defend their offspring resonates as the greatest of struggles, igniting within them a lion-like roar of protection.

CH 1. Reflections

Possible Outcomes and Perspectives

My memoir outlines a profound personal journey through legal and spiritual challenges. Here, we will explore potential outcomes and perspectives from others.

1. Regardless of the legal outcome, my experiences gained significant personal growth and spiritual enlightenment. The challenges faced by me served as crucible, strengthening my faith and resolve. This internal transformation enables me to find new ways to support and protect my child's education and well-being, perhaps through grassroots community efforts or by forming support networks for other parents facing similar struggles.

2. Despite my best efforts, this legal battle results in a partial victory, where the court recognizes some of their grievances but doesn't grant all requested relief. This outcome leads me to become a vocal advocate for educational reform and parental rights, using my experience to rally community support and drive long-term change.

3. I have successfully navigated the legal challenges posed by the Somerset County Board of Education, resulting in a court ruling that not only supports my right to homeschool my child but also prompts a review and reform of local education policies. This outcome underscores the power of faith and perseverance in enacting positive change within the community.

Chapter 2

Though my encounter with the Bailiff occurred months later, I was already consumed with gathering evidence to support my child's education, from emails to videos.

I meticulously organized my youngest child's educational materials, keeping her schoolwork neatly stored in a binder and notebook. This included her assignments in Bible Poetry, Science, History, and Math, all in the binder, while her Reading assignments were documented in a black and white composition book. Both the composition book and the binder housed her Language Arts Assignments.

Opting for a private homeschool program allowed us the freedom to unschool our child, enabling her to learn at her own pace and explore the world around her.

In the face of community and local school system harassment, I understood the importance of staying ahead of the system's potential challenges. To safeguard against any attempts to undermine our educational choices, I diligently documented every assignment completed by my child, providing thorough evidence of her progress. This proactive approach stemmed from previous legal encounters, including a civil case against the Somerset County Board of Education and others for their alleged organized crimes.

Despite verbal communication and email exchanges with the Board of Education employees, including the individual who filed the complaint with the state of Maryland, I found myself served with legal action without any follow-up from the State's Attorney since August 2023. This failure to uphold due process, particularly in ensuring the welfare of the child's education, underscored the negligence within the system. Numerous employees, including the student services employee and their supervisor, along with the superintendent, were implicated in this oversight.

Amidst the turmoil, I gathered the green binder and black and white notebook containing my child's completed educational assignments, a tangible representation of our unwavering commitment to her education.

During these preparations, unexpected events unfolded.

A shadow outside hinted at my husband's return, but instead, it revealed a tow truck reclaiming his vehicle. I panicked, convinced it was a setup, only to discover the car was merely parked inoperable. Stress mounted as challenges compounded.

Despite the chaos, I remained focused. Armed with my child's schoolwork, I confronted the Somerset County District Courts, disproving allegations of truancy with meticulous documentation spanning months. With each piece of evidence, I fortified my defense against unjust accusations.

In the midst of handling legal matters, I encountered resistance at the clerk's office but persisted in ensuring all necessary documents were copied, even my daughter's school assignments. Though not obligated to prove her education, I felt compelled to showcase our commitment. Retrieving forgotten originals heightened my mistrust of the court system, prompting a motion for their return. Surprisingly, they arrived promptly by mail. Amidst these challenges, including another vehicle towing, I found solace in prayer, recognizing divine intervention amidst the chaos. Despite the storm of events, my gratitude and faith sustained me, especially with my birthday and Christmas approaching, reminding me that with God, nothing is impossible.

In the memoir of our journey guided by faith, amidst the Christmas season, my husband and I faced a pivotal decision—to let one vehicle remain in repo while reclaiming another. Yet, in the midst of uncertainty, we found solace in God's presence, knowing He provides for our needs. As we ventured to retrieve our vehicle, adorned with the stark label of "repo," I couldn't help but see it as a testament to our journey—a journey marked by reliance on God's grace. Despite financial strain and looming challenges, I remained steadfast, trusting in God's plan. However, as the new year unfolded, a court hearing on January 16, 2024, for an alleged violation of Maryland Education Code 7-301 cast a shadow of uncertainty over our lives. Armed with evidence and faith, I believed justice would prevail—but reality had a different outcome, ushering in a new chapter of trials and resilience.

While awaiting the initial hearing, I searched for and gathered more evidence to include with the school work documents that was previously provided to the courts. This evidence had to prove that the case should be dismissed without me actually documenting dismissed. There were no evidence to show that I failed to send my child to school and I had evidence that I didn't fail through notifying the Board of Education.

Much time was consumed searching through my iCloud and email for photos, videos, and emails to provide evidence of the verbal explanation and email explanation. To be more in depth with the information provided, I even included information from the previous court case I had against the Somerset County Board of Education to support that this was a retaliatory case.

By any means, I put all videos and images within a thumb drive and supplied copies of the emails found. All emails were provided except for the main email that I needed to show proof that I indeed emailed the point of contacts at the Board of Education this information. I kept searching and typing key terms but the information was missing as it if I could have deleted such information. I made my second big trip to provided the courts with what evidence, I had because no matter what it showed that my child was indeed getting the education she needed.

All I knew was that now, I was awaiting the initial hearing of this juvenile trial that is also called truancy court. The laws of truancy court is made to be misconstrued and confusing as the terminology of the court of law is deemed confusing especially for one to represent themselves in a court case. As a reminder, I could not afford a lawyer, but also was not eligible to receive a public defender. In the state of Maryland, public defenders are available to families in juvenile courts.

Granted, I have not applied for this assistance, but I knew the outcome of a previous request for a fee waiver for one of my other civil cases against the local government and was denied. I did not want to waste my time to apply for a public defender and already knew I was going to be denied.

I just knew that with all of the evidence I had, the case was going to be dropped. I knew that I was going to beat all of the odds against me. There was no way that this case was going to continue.

Until I read the name of the Judge that will be hearing the case.

I could hear the anxiety from the pupulations of my heart pounding. I began to question myself and question the intent of the case. All seemed so surreal. This definitely was a retaliatory case. I thought to myself "all odds are against me."

As the civil case against the Somerset County Board of Education loomed, I found myself facing a familiar dilemma: a judge I had previously moved to recuse was once again presiding over my case. Despite the tight deadline, I couldn't find the time to file for recusal, and I also wanted to confront the judge in person.

The night before my court hearing, I frantically searched through my emails, desperately seeking proof that I had notified the Board of Education about my child's enrollment in private schooling. Amidst my search, I stumbled upon the crucial email, and relief washed over me.

The next morning, I rose early to prepare myself and my youngest child for court. With little support, as I was representing myself, I embarked on the short drive to the courthouse.

The drive to the court was very short, leading us to the location where my husband typically parks, situated on the side where the Town Office, Fire Department, State's Attorney's office, employees, and the Sheriff's parking lot are located. This spot is perpendicular to 30512 Prince William St. Princess Anne, MD 21853. Specifically, we were parked on Church Street, across from the government buildings and adjacent to the open fenced trash area for the courthouse. My husband favored this spot as he was the one driving. My husband opted to run a quick errand.   The thoughts of my husband uplifted me somewhat since he has aversions to legal battles, believing the case unnecessary since the Board of Education had been informed of the change.

Arriving at the courthouse, I encountered a sheriff acting as a bailiff, insisting that I lock away my cellphone. Despite my protests, I reluctantly complied due to time constraints. As I entered the courthouse with my youngest daughter, I couldn't shake the feeling of being caught up in this legal ordeal.

After filing a motion and submitting the supplemental evidence, a sense of accomplishment washed over me. Yet, as I waited in the courtroom, surrounded by a handful of others with "similar" legal matters, my nerves began to fray.

With a handful of cases scheduled for the day, the wait for the judge felt interminable. Finally, my husband arrived, bringing a semblance of support amidst the tension.

As I gazed at the judge, a mix of emotions swirled within me. This was the moment I had been dreading and anticipating – facing the very judge who had dismissed and mooted my motions for a previously filed civil case against the Plaintiffs. Despite my mistrust and apprehension, I braced myself for what lay ahead, knowing that my fight for justice was far from over. In that instant, I realized that only God could save me from the legal complexities of this case.

CH 2. Reflections

Possible Outcomes and Perspectives

My memoir outlines a profound personal journey through legal and spiritual challenges. Here, we will explore potential outcomes and perspectives from others.

1. As the judge reviews the evidence I presented, including the crucial email proving I had notified the Board of Education, he will acknowledge the validity of my claims. The judge rules in my favor, dismissing the case against me. Relieved and elated, I leave the courthouse with my husband and daughter, grateful that the ordeal has come to a favorable end. This experience strengthens my resolve to be more meticulous with important documents and reinforces my belief in the justice system.

2.The judge listens to my arguments and examines the evidence, but finds that additional documentation is needed to fully support my case. He will decide to postpone the hearing, giving me a set time to gather and submit the required evidence. Although disappointed by the delay, I feel a sense of determination to gather all necessary information and return to court prepared. My husband's continued support helps me stay optimistic as I work through the additional legal requirements.

3. Despite my efforts and the evidence presented, the judge is not convinced that the notification to the Board of Education was adequately communicated or timely. The ruling goes against me, possibly resulting in a fine or other consequences. This outcome leaves me feeling disheartened and frustrated with the legal system. However, I resolve to consult with a legal professional for any future legal matters, ensuring that I am better prepared and represented if similar situations arise.

Chapter 3

The roll call for each case commenced with the announcement of case numbers and defendants' names. After confirming attendance, the judge ushered everyone into his presence, marking the start of the hearing for all defendants. As the judge began reciting our rights and the charge of "failure to send a child to school," I found myself staring blankly, attempting to discern his intentions. His lack of acknowledgment felt like a deliberate avoidance, possibly stemming from resentment over my recusal from a civil case, rendering it moot.

Amidst the enumeration of penalties under Md Education Code 703.1 – jail time, fines, community service – I steeled myself for the outcome, whether failure or success in my defense. Armed with evidence, I was prepared for the day's proceedings.

Expecting to present my case solo, I was surprised when the judge instructed me to sign a document affirming my understanding of my right to legal representation and its consequences, which he reiterated verbally. To my dismay, instead of presenting my evidence, I was informed that I would have to return for an adjudicative court hearing on February 16, 2024. My case remained unresolved, despite my readiness and evidence.

After leaving the courthouse, I was overwhelmed with a sense of defeat, feeling as though I had reached a point of no return. The prolonged court proceedings left my youngest child bewildered, prompting me to explain it simply as a matter involving the government and her school. However, my husband grew frustrated with my reaction, insisting the case was unnecessary given our evidence.

While I comprehended his perspective, it was the underlying motive behind the case that fueled my frustration with the system. I acknowledge the importance of education and strive for my children to excel, evident in my oldest child's academic achievements as a early graduate student for the 2023-2024 school year and full-ride scholarship to the University of Maryland. Yet, she has not received the recognition she deserves.

My commitment to advocating for my children's success knows no bounds. Yet, I've encountered educational challenges since relocating to this county in 2018, where cultural standards seem to restrict minority individuals from rising without conforming. The lack of diversity within the courthouse personnel further underscores this disparity.

Despite these obstacles, I entrust my children's futures to a higher power, praying for strength to overcome societal barriers. I refuse to succumb to defeat, recognizing my role as a beacon of resilience for my daughters. Despite the looming threat of incarceration, I persisted, taking solace in educating my child at home while preparing for the next hearing.

Internally, I felt the school system was encroaching on my parental rights, attempting to dictate my child's education. Nevertheless, I remained steadfast in my approach, continuing to educate my youngest child amidst the legal turmoil.

Allow me to share a glimpse into my life. As a stay-at-home mother, I found myself embroiled in a battle against the government after refusing to accept a deal following harassment in the workplace. Despite reporting the incidents, I became a target for higher-level bullying and surveillance. Living among coworkers and families associated with these crimes only intensified the ordeal.

My focus shifted to protecting my youngest child after she experienced targeting at preschool, leading to a civil case against the school system when she was just three years old. Now, at six, the hurt lingers, compounded by the government's failure to address their wrongdoing.

Once a supporter of the system, I now find myself disillusioned and distrusting. Yet, guided by faith, I believe there's a purpose in my struggle, a reason to stand against corruption. My resolve to fight for my family remains unwavering, even as I grapple with anger and paranoia instilled by the government's actions.

With each day, I confront the injustice, seeking solace in prayer and the strength to endure. Despite the tarnishing of my reputation within the community, I find resilience in knowing I stand against a powerful adversary.

Navigating an arduous court case, I realized the importance of proper legal terminology and research, empowering me to present my defense with confidence. Despite the intimidation tactics, I remained steadfast, armed with evidence and a thorough understanding of my rights.

As I entered the courtroom for the adjudicative hearing, I felt a mix of apprehension and determination. Despite the presence of familiar faces intent on undermining my case, I remained focused, determined to seek justice for myself and my family.

In the face of adversity, I refuse to be silenced or intimidated. With faith as my guide, I press forward, knowing that truth and perseverance will prevail in the end.

After a brief wait, the State prosecutor arrived in the court hallway for roll call. Despite being called last again, I responded, only to learn that more time was needed for their witnesses. This unexpected delay left my husband and me puzzled and frustrated. Despite the uncertainty, we patiently awaited our turn to enter the courtroom.

As we waited, the anticipation of presenting my case lingered in my mind, overshadowed by the need for more time by the State's attorney. Finally, when called, we entered the courtroom.

Inside, I observed the judge, using a different name label, and various personnel present. Despite distractions, I remained focused on presenting my case. The judge reiterated my rights and the extension request, which left me appalled. Introducing others present, including a public defender and school personnel, further fueled my frustration.

Leaving the courtroom, I felt disgraced by the delay, compounded by the judge scheduling the next hearing on my youngest child's birthday. Reflecting on the justice system's motives, I declined school paperwork offered, knowing my parental rights. The judge's mention of 'jail' instead of alternatives intensified my concerns about the system's injustices.

Leaving the courthouse, I declined my husband's suggestion to walk home due to the cold, opting to call my mom for a ride. Filled with rage, I shared my anguish with my husband, showing him my summary and evidence.

When my mother arrived, my daughter's joy lifted my spirits momentarily. However, thoughts of potential incarceration lingered, prompting me to cherish every moment with my family. Now, we face the wait for the next court date, coinciding with my child's birthday, with overwhelming anticipation and a prayer for divine intervention.

CH 3. Reflections

Possible Outcomes and Perspectives

My memoir outlines a profound personal journey through legal and spiritual challenges. Here, we will explore potential outcomes and perspectives from others.

1. Despite being prepared to present evidence, I face continued delays with my case being postponed to an adjudicative hearing on February 16, 2024. This prolongs the legal process and leaves the me in a state of uncertainty and frustration, impacting my emotional well-being and family dynamics.

2. The unresolved court case and prolonged proceedings lead to tension and disagreement within my family. My husband is frustrated and believes the case is unnecessary given our evidence, while I feel overwhelmed and defeated. This discord highlights the emotional and relational strain caused by the legal battle.

3. I remain committed to advocating for my children's success and addressing systemic challenges within the educational and legal systems. Despite feeling frustrated with the lack

of recognition and support, particularly for minority individuals, I continue to strive for equity and excellence in education, reflecting broader issues of cultural and institutional barriers.

Chapter 4

Amidst everything and before my upcoming court case, I initiated legal action against a military individual to obtain government information regarding surveillance of my home and travels. During this process, I encountered an imposter posing as a government official. The reference case numbers for these incidents are as follows: D022CV24808102, D022CV24808106, D022CV24808099, D022CV24808100, D022CV24808103, D022CV24808105.

Subsequently, I filed a peace order detailing the situation. However, faced with familiar challenges, including having previously recused the judge, the odds were once again against me. This occurred in the district court, where I had previously filed other civil cases.

I was disheartened when the judge dismissed the claim of electronic harassment, citing the military man's residence in a different state and his potential assistance, regardless of his true identity. The judge directed me to address the matter with the commissioners, stating it wasn't within her purview to issue peace orders for legal matters. As a result, the peace order was denied, and the case was dismissed.

Feeling overwhelmed by the injustices of the court, I experienced a mental breakdown. Upon leaving without a copy of the filed documents, I returned only to be followed by a female bailiff, which heightened my distress. In a moment of anger and frustration, I vocalized my discontent, intentionally disturbing the peace to express my emotions. Despite my repeated demands to be taken to jail, the staff members assured me that I wasn't disrupting the peace.

As the situation escalated, I continued expressing my frustration in the hallway. When the male supervisor bailiff asked for my name to file a complaint, I questioned his authority and insisted on knowing his name, asserting my rights. However, his dismissive response and denial of my rights further exacerbated the situation, leading to a tense exchange.

The moment when it became clear that someone within the government was stripping away my rights ignited a profound anger within me. As I demanded answers, the attempts to silence me only confirmed my suspicions that there was more to the story.

Reflecting on the legal proceedings that had shifted against me, from being the plaintiff to defending myself, I couldn't shake the feeling that the system had failed to protect my human and civil rights.

Delving into the background of the corruption surrounding the circuit court judge presiding over my truancy case, I uncovered troubling connections to the military and law enforcement. His past roles as a military man and state attorney, focused on assisting police rather than civilians, raised serious questions about conflicts of interest.

The case I had filed against the Town of Princess Anne and Somerset County Public Schools exposed falsified police reports, the harm inflicted on my child in public school, and subsequent retaliation in the community. Many law enforcement and legal professionals have ties to the military, forming organizations like the Fraternal Order of Police and the VFW Post, where they discuss targets and prioritize their own interests over serving the community.

In a discovered filed police report, one of the police officers mentioned was an organizer of the Fraternal Order of Police. When I was informed by the Bailiff that I had no rights, it was this officer who escorted me out of the courthouse during a moment of rage. His attempt to console me only fueled my anger further, as I confronted him about allegedly falsifying police reports and questioned his trustworthiness. Despite denying any involvement in such reports, I had evidence to the contrary, which seemed to unsettle him. A mental health vehicle arrived, but the officer waved them off, indicating he was aware that I had uncovered his deceit.

In the following weeks, as I prepared to present my case, I struggled with overwhelming mental health issues exacerbated by the corruption I faced. Despite my distress, my husband's focus was on work rather than supporting my well-being, leaving me feeling abandoned. I sought assistance from the courts, filing a complaint against the Bailiff for his dismissive behavior.

As I prepared for my court case, the threat of jail loomed over me, prompting me to consider drastic measures rather than surrendering my child to the flawed school system. While I was not physically coerced, the legal proceedings felt like a retaliatory force, devoid of proper due process.

As I delved deeper into the intricacies of truancy laws, I encountered a maze of legal jargon that left my mind ablaze. It's no wonder it takes years to become proficient in law; deciphering its complexities requires dedication and perseverance.

Yet, I discovered that with the right tools and determination, understanding the law's nuances is attainable. This realization marked the beginning of a transformation in my legal approach. Filing motions became second nature, each one meticulously crafted to leverage the law in my favor.

As I gained a deeper understanding, I noticed a shift in the court's demeanor towards my case. The administrators and clerks attempted to intimidate me, but their tactics only fueled my determination. From delaying copy charges to fabricating names, they resorted to desperate measures to impede my progress.

But I refused to be deterred. Armed with a newfound understanding of the law, I navigated through their tactics with ease. The tables turned as the laws were wielded to expose the flaws in their case and demand a fair trial.

My efforts did not go unnoticed by the court, the state's attorney's office, or even the sheriff's acting as Baliff. Despite their attempts to undermine me, I remained steadfast in my pursuit of justice.

However, their discrimination reared its ugly head when they dismissed me as needing a 'public defender,' a presumptuous and biased assumption based on my minority status and unique name. This discrimination only fueled my determination to prove them wrong.

Though I may not have had the means to hire a lawyer, I refused to be silenced. My journey through the legal system, fraught with challenges and discrimination, is a testament to the resilience of the human spirit in the face of injustice.

Overall, I felt a sense of unsettling triumph, knowing I was getting under their skin. It became imperative to defend my case truthfully, yet I also held onto the belief that divine justice would prevail, causing our adversaries to falter without our intentional malice. Amidst the tension, I endeavored to maintain composure and extend courtesy.

I pressed on, asserting my rights as a self-represented individual, insisting on access to the necessary information. In the backdrop, I recognized the leverage of potentially extending the trial or even dismissing the case due to violations of due process rights, which were apparent from the outset. There was a glaring lack of follow-up regarding my child's school attendance, the failure to file motions for witness extensions, and unmet requests for evidence.

As the court date loomed, I found myself scrambling for crucial information while encountering a bewildering dance with the circuit judge's clerk and staff, who seemed to vacillate on the visibility and scheduling of my case. Amidst this bureaucratic labyrinth, I maintained my calm demeanor, understanding that the clerk's potential displeasure with my motions may have contributed to the chaos.

The unsettling revelation of the main clerk's familial ties to criminal activities within the community added another layer of complexity. Their involvement, along with that of their relatives and associates, in elaborate criminal schemes against me and potential restrictions on accessing my files, likely fueled a vindictive motive among the staff. Despite these adversities, I remained steadfast and composed.

It's the week of my court case, and I'm unsure if it will be heard. I haven't received updates on the status of my motions—whether they were denied, moot, or accepted. Given past experiences, I assumed they were denied and moot, as has been the trend.

Despite this, I knew my due process rights entitled me to evidence for proper preparation. Despite initial hurdles with the state attorney's office, they eventually provided the requested information, albeit after some insistence on my rights.

Upon following up with the courts, I was informed that the case still existed, but accessing the court docket online proved challenging until the day before the hearing.

Aware of the courts' new policy charging for copies of filed motions, I spent the night before the hearing making copies for myself, the plaintiffs, and the judge. My preparations lasted all night, including printing the court docket for review. However, it was during this review that I discovered crucial information that hadn't been communicated to me despite multiple attempts to contact the courts. This revelation was confirmed when I arrived for the adjudicative hearing, leaving me astonished.

CH 4. Reflections

Possible Outcomes and Perspectives

My memoir outlines a profound personal journey through legal and spiritual challenges. Here, we will explore potential outcomes and perspectives from others.

1. I may choose to appeal the dismissal of the peace order and the judge's refusal to address the electronic harassment claim. If the appeal is successful, a higher court could overturn the previous decision, mandate a re-evaluation of my claims, or remand the case for further proceedings. This could provide another opportunity for my allegations to be properly considered.

2. Another possible outcome is to file a formal complaint against the judge and court officials involved in my case. This could lead to an investigation by judicial oversight bodies or commissions, which might result in disciplinary actions against those officials if misconduct or bias is found. Additionally, such a complaint could bring attention to systemic issues within the court system.

3.   I could pursue legal action for emotional distress and violations of your civil rights. This could involve suing for damages due to the mental breakdown and distress caused by the court's handling of my case. If successful, this could lead to compensation and possibly policy changes to prevent similar occurrences in the future.

Chapter 5

Courage Under Pressure: A Mother's Journey Through Justice on Her Daughter's Birthday

On the day of my court case, coincidentally also my baby girl's birthday, I found myself balancing the anticipation of celebrating her special day with the looming prospect of potential jail time. Despite the judge's calculated timing to unsettle me, I was resolute in defending my daughter and myself against the system.

Preparing both my youngest daughter and myself for the day ahead, I decided to surprise the court by wearing a "Mom of the Birthday Girl" shirt and bringing my eldest daughter along as a witness, demonstrating our commitment to education and punctuality. Armed with evidence spanning multiple school years, I ensured my daughters were fed and ready before heading to court.

While my youngest daughter was excited for her birthday and the court proceedings, I couldn't shake the weight of uncertainty regarding my future. I had to explain to her the possibility of me missing her birthday due to jail time, a conversation that highlighted the harsh realities of our situation. Nonetheless, I encouraged her to enjoy her birthday weekend, reassuring her that I had plans in place, even if I couldn't be there.

As we waited in the car for my husband and eldest daughter to join us, I reflected on the challenges I had faced in recent months and the unique protection I felt from a higher power. My journey to navigate the legal system as a minority had been arduous, requiring extensive research and perseverance.

Upon arrival at the courthouse, we adhered to the strict security protocols, including locking our phones in a clear lock, much to my eldest daughter's surprise. The encounter with the bailiff further escalated tensions, with his unusual line of questioning and handling of our belongings adding to the strain of the day.

The male sheriff acting as the bailiff immediately engaged in a series of inquiries, unlike his usual routine. His question about the courtroom seemed oddly prescient, signaling his awareness of my case. Despite my attempt to assert my knowledge of his recognition, the situation intensified as he fumbled for his clipboard, indicating he would request my name, although he had already informed me of my car's location. This led to a tense exchange, exacerbated by his repetitive questioning of my daughters. Asserting my parental rights, I intervened on their behalf, which further aggravated the situation.

As I proceeded through the metal detector, the bailiff mishandled my belongings, causing my evidence to spill. Insisting he refrain from touching my items without a warrant, I eventually navigated through the security process. Despite my initial concern that he may have tampered with my evidence, it was ultimately found intact in the box. With my daughters in tow, I regrouped before heading upstairs to address my case.

Despite the setbacks, I remained determined to present my case effectively. Sorting through the disarray summary, and evidence caused by the bailiff, I ensured all evidence was intact before proceeding to the courtroom with my daughters in tow.

As I ascended the stairs, I encountered a larger group than usual awaiting court proceedings. Carrying a heavy box of documents, I felt its weight increase with each step. After a chaotic few minutes with the Bailiff, organizing my materials, and hauling the box upstairs, we were finally ushered into the courtroom. Exhausted, I took a moment to catch my breath and smiled at my daughters, silently apologizing to them and seeking forgiveness from God for any embarrassment they may have felt witnessing my actions. I wanted to teach them the importance of standing up for their rights, no matter the circumstances.

As we waited for the judge, my husband joined us, displaying impatience despite arriving late as usual. Time felt particularly significant that day, as it was our youngest child's seventh birthday. Despite my desire to celebrate at home, I was prepared to face jail time to shield her from the injustices we've endured as a family. Amidst the soft murmurings of other court attendees, I anxiously awaited the judge's arrival.

When the judge finally entered, confirming the unsettling reality of what I had seen on the docket the night before, I was overcome with disbelief. The surreal became all too real.

As my case transitioned to a new judge, a female this time, I found myself charting unfamiliar territory. The previous judge's bias had been evident, but with this new one, uncertainty loomed. Her name hadn't resonated in any courtroom across the Tri-County Maryland area where my case had been heard. Anticipation gripped me as the roll call progressed, my name conspicuously absent, despite knowing I'd been marked present by a case witness. While I had braced myself to confront the previous judge's hostility, I now faced a different challenge. With every participant preceding me, the weight of anticipation grew. It was evident that the judicial staff aimed to keep my case low-profile.

Yet, armed with unique evidence, I was determined to make my case heard. As the new judge, a woman, finally called my name, doubts and questions swirled in my mind. Was I truly prepared? Was this the moment to lay bare my case's essence?

CH 5. Reflections

My memoir outlines a profound personal journey through legal and spiritual challenges. Here, we will explore potential outcomes and perspectives from others.

1. The judge could decide whether my evidence that was mishandled by the bailiff should be admitted in court. The judge's decision will significantly impact the case's outcome, either benefiting or disadvantaging my position.

2. The experience of navigating the chaotic court process, coupled with the emotional strain of the day on my represented child's birthday, could have lasting emotional effects on my family, especially my children. My actions and the court's proceedings could influence my children's perception of justice and my family's resilience.

3. Depending on how the court proceedings unfold, I could face various legal outcomes, such as having my case dismissed, winning my argument, or facing jail time. My willingness to go to jail to protect my children underscores the

high stakes and potential for a dramatic resolution.

Chapter 6

As I stood before the judge, ready to present my case, I couldn't help but notice the prosecutor's preparedness, flanked by her witness. The gravity of the moment hit me; it was time to speak up.

Questions flooded my mind. Where should I begin? How does this process unfold? I understood that the plaintiff would start with their statements. As these thoughts swirled, I found myself listening to the judge's explanation of her rulings on my motions.

She informed me of her decisions, including the denial of most motions and the mootness of one. I acknowledged her instructions, expressing my intent to file a motion to recuse the judge. My goal was to shed light on perceived injustices and partiality toward law enforcement in this case.

The judge reiterated the claims against me, emphasizing the penalties I faced under the law. Despite pressure from the state's attorney to settle by signing a homeschooling document, I remained steadfast. This was not about signing papers; it was about defending my rights and my child's education.

When the judge hinted at the consequences of refusing to settle, including potential jail time, I stood firm. I was prepared to face whatever outcome awaited, knowing deep down that signing those documents wasn't an option.

As proceedings resumed, I took on the role of representing myself and my family. It was daunting, yet empowering, to fight for justice despite my past. The questioning of the plaintiff's witness revealed irrelevant details, focusing more on administrative lapses than the crux of the matter.

When my turn came to question the witness, I initially stumbled, mixing statements with inquiries. The judge's guidance helped me refocus, honing in on the crucial question: the email confirming my child's enrollment in private schooling, sent on August 7, 2023.

During the court proceedings, I questioned the witness about an email I had sent, to which she claimed she hadn't received. Despite providing a copy of the email as evidence, the plaintiff objected. However, after the judge reviewed the evidence, it was accepted. When I inquired if her colleagues had mentioned the email, she denied any knowledge. This lack of response from the recipients left me wondering if my emails were being ignored, intercepted, or redirected.

I maintained my belief that the emails were received, given the absence of bounce-backs and my assumption that someone at their facility had read them. Presenting another email from February 2023 resulted in a similar objection from the plaintiff, which was overruled by the judge upon review.

The judge noted the repeated claim of the witness not receiving my emails and suggested signing the documents as requested. However, I stood firm, asserting that doing so would compromise my parental rights and the educational choices I've made for my child.

Despite the focus on signing documents, I emphasized that the core issue should be the alleged failure to send. It became evident that the state's attorney was pushing for document signing rather than addressing the original matter.

Even when the judge expressed reluctance to send me to jail solely for refusing to sign, I reiterated my willingness to face consequences to defend my rights. The judge's concern about the intent behind signing the document was evident.

Ultimately, the judge requested documents for review and questioned the witnesses about the service of documents for the current school year. They confirmed that all necessary information was included in the packet on the judge's podium.

The judge reviewed the information and expressed concern over my willingness to face jail time rather than sign a document. As she asked questions from the homeschool packet, it wasn't until the third question that I broke down in tears, feeling compelled to do something I found unsettling and unjustified.

Despite answering the judge's questions, I preferred jail time over what I saw as an unjust situation, having mentally prepared for this moment for months. While knowing I would miss my family, especially my baby girls, I was resolved to do what I felt was right.

However, the atmosphere began to change as I questioned the judge about the paperwork. She explained the yearly requirement for homeschool documentation and suggested mailing instead of emailing. Eventually, she proposed completing the documents together in court in August, ensuring the state attorney and the witness agreed.

Reflecting on the situation, I couldn't help but wonder why this willingness to accommodate hadn't been present earlier, especially when my evidence of private school attendance was initially disregarded. Now, we circled back to that topic, with the understanding that the witness would review the homeschool provisions after I completed and signed the documents.

My faith in God was solidified when the judge, upon reviewing the evidence of my child's homeschool program, swiftly dismissed the case without any need for further documentation or signatures. It was a moment where God's intervention was palpable, turning what seemed like imminent jail time into a testimony of divine protection.

The state attorney's frustration was evident as she abruptly left the courtroom, and the judge, recognizing the achievements of my daughters, extended warm wishes to my family. Her compassion and commitment to justice amidst prevailing corruption left an indelible mark on my heart.

As we left, there was a subtle confrontation with court staff who had expected a different outcome, but their disbelief couldn't overshadow the righteousness of our case.

On the journey home, amidst the relief, my family expressed their concern, wondering why I refused to sign the document and risk going to jail. However, there was a deeper reason at play - divine intervention. By studying the laws and invoking the 'stand your ground' principle, I held onto hope. Considering the consequences if I had signed, would the truth ever come to light in this corrupt county and community?

I share this experience in the hope that it inspires others facing similar challenges to hold onto hope and trust in God's plan. The journey may be arduous, but with faith, justice can prevail. David in Psalm 37 bears witness to this truth from God.

As I reflect, I'm drawn to thoughts of unanswered emails and denied requests, like the one for a trial by jury for a fair trial. Yet, for now, it's time to celebrate my youngest daughter's birthday and my oldest daughter's achievements.

CH 6. Reflections

Possible Outcomes and Perspectives

My memoir outlines a profound personal journey through legal and spiritual challenges. Here, we will explore potential outcomes and perspectives from others.

1. Despite the judge's initial expression of concern and my emotional response, the case could proceed with further legal proceedings. I might continue to face challenges, including potential jail time, if a resolution isn't reached. This outcome underscores the ongoing tension between my convictions and the legal system's requirements, highlighting the complexities of navigating such disputes.

2. The judge proposes a compromise where I agree to complete the necessary homeschool documentation in court, with the state attorney and witness present to ensure all legal requirements are met. This outcome provides a resolution that satisfies legal requirements while acknowledging the my stance and willingness to cooperate under certain conditions.

3. The judge, after reviewing the evidence of the homeschool program and understanding my sincerity and preparedness, dismisses the case without requiring further documentation or signatures. This outcome reflects a recognition of the my efforts and the validity of the homeschool program, leading to a favorable resolution without the need for punitive measures.

Final Results

Possible Outcomes and Perspectives

My memoir outlines a profound personal journey through legal and spiritual challenges. Here, we will explore my outcome and perspective.

Not everyone has a fair chance at challenging the legal system, especially when representing oneself as a woman of color who is often labeled as the "angry black woman" of the community. I would rather be seen this way and maintain my integrity than conform to what the system wants me to be. I was willing to risk being another minority in jail to fight for my children's educational rights. This was about me and my family, and I stood firm in my beliefs. I was not going to allow my child to continue being harmed by the school system. Without God's guidance in my life, I wouldn't have received a fair and impartial trial. But I persevered and was able to celebrate my now 7-year-old's birthday and, in the future, my oldest child's early graduation. These milestones are to be cherished forever. Who knows? Another retaliatory case might be brought against me after the release of this book. I pray that my journey inspires someone.

Appendices
Authentic Images

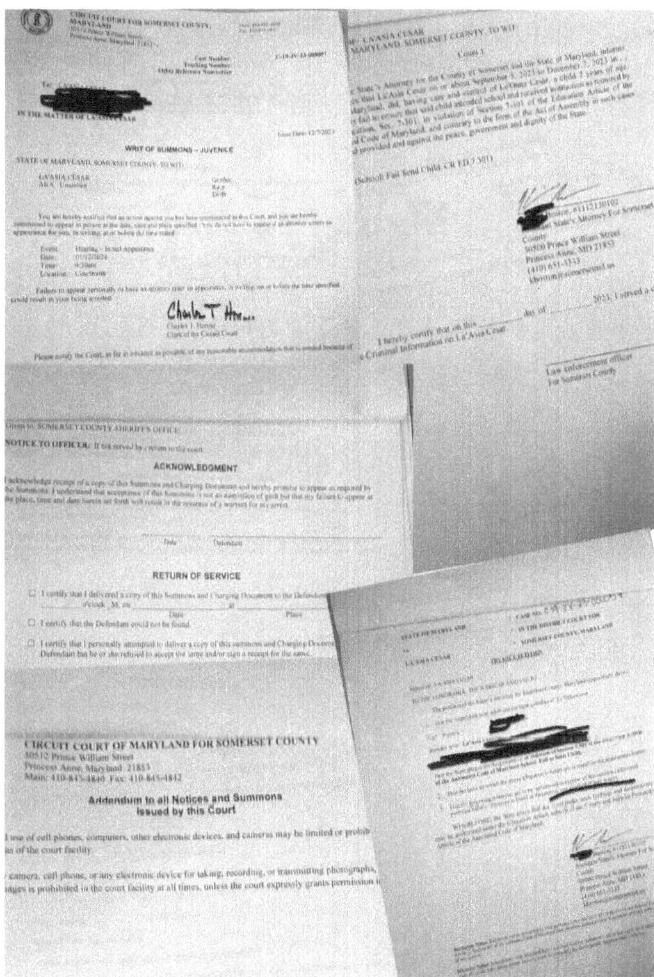

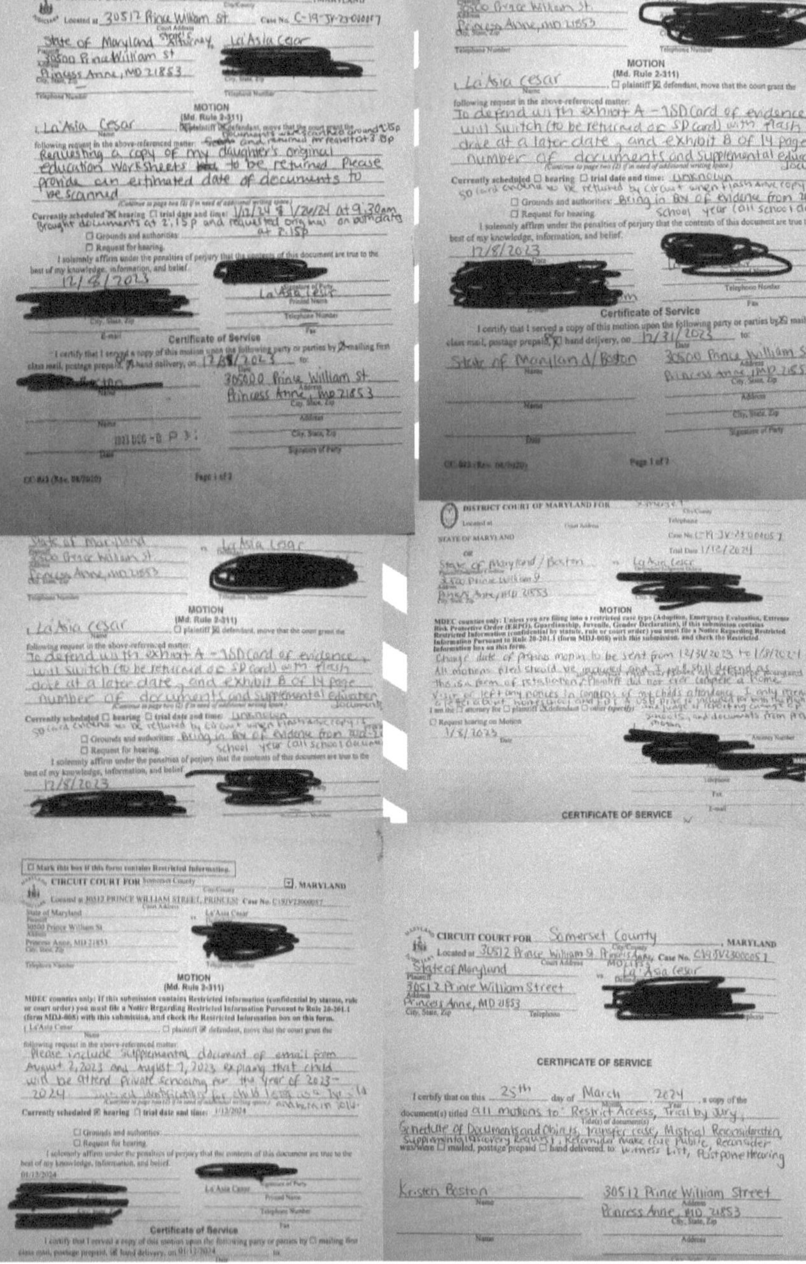

CIRCUIT COURT FOR Somerset, **MARYLAND**
Located at 30512 Prince William St. Case No. C-19-JV-23-000057
State of Maryland State's Attorney vs. La'Asia Cesar
30500 Prince William St
Princess Anne, MD 21853

MOTION
(Md. Rule 2-311)
I, La'Asia Cesar, plaintiff / defendant, move that the court grant the following request in the above-referenced matter: Documents were scanned around 2:15p and returned per request at 3:15p Requesting a copy of my daughter's original education worksheets to be returned. Please provide an estimated date of documents to be scanned

Currently scheduled hearing / trial date and time: 1/12/24 & 1/26/24 at 9:30am Brought documents at 2:15p and requested original on both dates at 2:15p

I solemnly affirm under the penalties of perjury that the contents of this document are true to the best of my knowledge, information, and belief.
12/8/2023
La'Asia Cesar

State of Maryland
3500 Prince William St.
Princess Anne, MD 21853 vs. La'Asia Cesar

MOTION
(Md. Rule 2-311)
I, La'Asia Cesar, plaintiff / defendant, move that the court grant the following request in the above-referenced matter: To defend with exhibit A – 1SD card of evidence, will switch (to be returned as SD card) with flash drive at a later date, and exhibit B of 14 page number of documents and supplemental education documents

Currently scheduled hearing / trial date and time: unknown SD card evidence to be returned by circuit when flash drive copy is provided

Grounds and authorities: Bring in box of evidence from 2023-20 school year (all school documents)

I solemnly affirm under the penalties of perjury that the contents of this document are true to the best of my knowledge, information, and belief.
12/8/2023

Certificate of Service
I certify that I served a copy of this motion upon the following party or parties by mailing first class mail, postage prepaid / hand delivery, on 12/31/2023 to:
State of Maryland/Boston 30500 Prince William St.
Princess Anne, MD 21853

State of Maryland
3500 Prince William St.
Princess Anne, MD 21853 vs. La'Asia Cesar

MOTION
(Md. Rule 2-311)
I, La'Asia Cesar, plaintiff / defendant, move that the court grant the following request in the above-referenced matter: To defend with exhibit A – 1SD card of evidence, will switch (to be returned as SD card) with flash drive at a later date, and exhibit B of 14 page number of documents and supplemental education documents

Currently scheduled hearing / trial date and time: unknown SD card evidence to be returned by circuit when flash drive copy is

Grounds and authorities: Bring in box of evidence from 2023-24 school year (all school documents)

I solemnly affirm under the penalties of perjury that the contents of this document are true to the best of my knowledge, information, and belief.
12/8/2023

DISTRICT COURT OF MARYLAND FOR
STATE OF MARYLAND Case No. C-19-JV-23-000057
OR Trial Date 1/12/2024
State of Maryland / Boston vs. La'Asia Cesar
3500 Prince William St.
Princess Anne, MD 21853

MOTION
MDEC counties only: Unless you are filing into a restricted case type (Adoption, Emergency Evaluation, Extreme Risk Protective Order (ERPO), Guardianship, Juvenile, Gender Declaration), if this submission contains Restricted Information (confidential by statute, rule or court order) you must file a Notice Regarding Restricted Information Pursuant to Rule 20-201.1 (form MDJ-008) with this submission, and check the Restricted Information box on this form.

Change date of previous motion to be sent from 12/31/2023 to 1/8/2024. All motions filed should be reviewed and I will still defend as this is a form of retaliation. Plaintiff did not ever complete a Home visit or left any notice in regards of my child's attendance. I only received classification at home and was told it is okay that I subbed for him in the subjects, and documents from plastic shoe

I am the attorney for plaintiff / defendant / other (specify)
Request hearing on Motion
1/8/2023

CERTIFICATE OF SERVICE

Mark this box if this form contains Restricted Information.
CIRCUIT COURT FOR Somerset County, **MARYLAND**
Located at 30512 PRINCE WILLIAM STREET, PRINCESS Case No. C19JV23000057
State of Maryland vs. La'Asia Cesar
30500 Prince William St.
Princess Anne, MD 21853

MOTION
(Md. Rule 2-311)
MDEC counties only: If this submission contains Restricted Information (confidential by statute, rule or court order) you must file a Notice Regarding Restricted Information Pursuant to Rule 20-201.1 (form MDJ-008) with this submission, and check the Restricted Information box on this form.
I, La'Asia Cesar, plaintiff / defendant, move that the court grant the following request in the above-referenced matter: Please include Supplemental document of email from August 2, 2023 and August 7, 2023 explaining that child will be attend private schooling for the year of 2023-2024. Initial notification for child sent as 2-Jul-14 notification in 2016+

Currently scheduled hearing / trial date and time: 1/13/2024

I solemnly affirm under the penalties of perjury that the contents of this document are true to the best of my knowledge, information, and belief.
01/13/2024
La'Asia Cesar

Certificate of Service
I certify that I served a copy of this motion upon the following party or parties by mailing first class mail, postage prepaid / hand delivery, on 01/13/2024 to:

CIRCUIT COURT FOR Somerset County, **MARYLAND**
Located at 30512 Prince William St. Princess Anne, MD 21853 Case No. C19JV23000057
State of Maryland vs. La'Asia Cesar
30512 Prince William Street
Princess Anne, MD 21853

CERTIFICATE OF SERVICE

I certify that on this 25th day of March 2024, a copy of the document(s) titled all motions to: Restrict Access, Trial by Jury, Signature of Documents and Objects, transfer case, Mistrial Reconsideration Supplemental Discovery Request, Reconsider make case public, Reconsider was/were mailed, postage prepaid / hand delivered to: Witness List, Postpone Hearing

Kristen Boston 30512 Prince William Street
Princess Anne, MD 21853

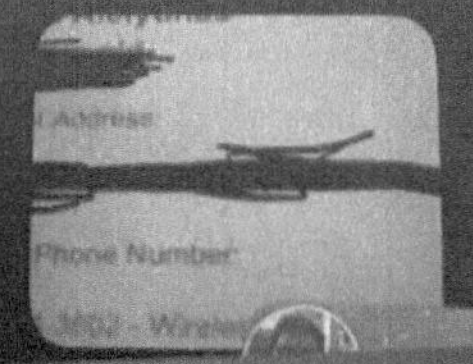

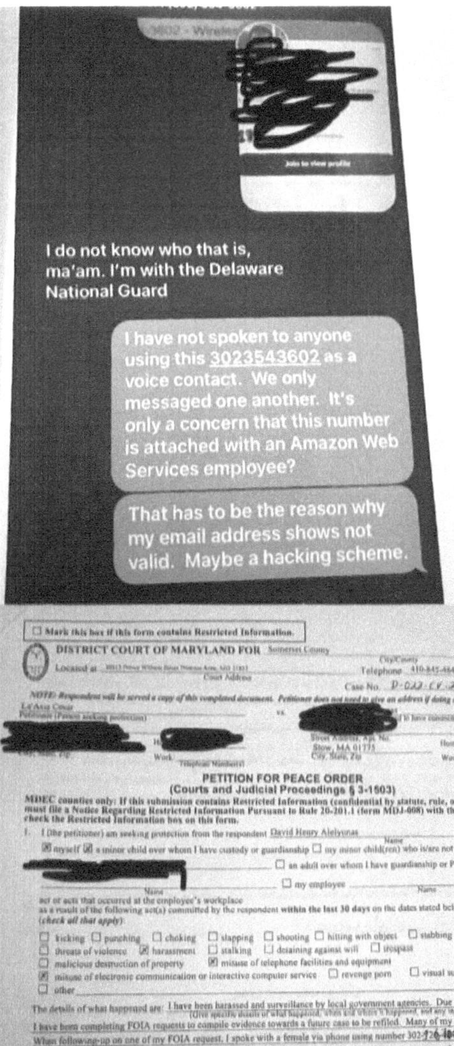

☐ Mark this box if this form contains Restricted Information.

DISTRICT COURT OF MARYLAND FOR Somerset County

Located at ___________________________
Court Address
City/County
Telephone 410-845-4840

Case No. D-022-CV-24

NOTE: Respondent will be served a copy of this completed document. Petitioner does not need to give an address if doing so

La'Asia Cesar
Petitioner (Person seeking protection)
vs.

Street Address, Apt. No.
Stow, MA 01775
City, State, Zip
Home
Work

PETITION FOR PEACE ORDER
(Courts and Judicial Proceedings § 3-1503)

MDEC counties only: If this submission contains Restricted Information (confidential by statute, rule, or must file a Notice Regarding Restricted Information Pursuant to Rule 20-201.1 (form MDJ-008) with this check the Restricted Information box on this form.

1. I (the petitioner) am seeking protection from the respondent David Henry Alelyunas
   Name
   ☒ myself ☒ a minor child over whom I have custody or guardianship ☐ my minor child(ren) who is/are not in
   ☐ an adult over whom I have guardianship or Pow
   ☐ my employee
   Name
   act or acts that occurred at the employee's workplace
   as a result of the following act(s) committed by the respondent **within the last 30 days** on the dates stated below
   (*check all that apply*):

   ☐ kicking ☐ punching ☐ choking ☐ slapping ☐ shooting ☐ hitting with object ☐ stabbing
   ☐ threats of violence ☒ harassment ☐ stalking ☐ detaining against will ☐ trespass
   ☐ malicious destruction of property ☒ misuse of telephone facilities and equipment
   ☒ misuse of electronic communication or interactive computer service ☐ revenge porn ☐ visual surv
   ☐ other ___________

   The details of what happened are: I have been harassed and surveillance by local government agencies. Due to
   (Give specific details of what happened, when and where it happened, and any injur
   I have been completing FOIA requests to compile evidence towards a future case to be refiled. Many of my ri
   When following-up on one of my FOIA request, I spoke with a female via phone using number 302-726-1810
   were from a different number of 302-354-3602. I messaged this number thinking it was the same person. I the
   number due to the number of harassment received and noticed that it belongs to David Alelyunas. When I exp
   Robert Alelyunas denied. I requested to complete a Facetime video, we completed one and it was unknowing

2. ☐ I am filing this petition on behalf of my minor child(ren) who is/are not in my custody. The minor ch
   care, custody or guardianship of: ___________
   Name
   Address

3. ☒ I am the legal guardian of the minor child(ren) for whom relief is sought. The parents of the child(ren) are:
   Child's Name
   Parent's Name
   Paren
   La'Asia Cesar
   La'Asia Cesar &

4. I know of the following court cases involving the respondent and the person(s) for whom I am seeking p

Court	Kind of Case	Year Filed	Results or

DC-PO-001 (Rev. 01/2024)
Page 1 of 2

Case Number: D022CV23007429/ C-19-CV-23-000139

1 of 3
L. Cesar
10/23/23

Dear J[redacted]

I am writing pursuant [redacted]
The judge has [redacted]
controversy;

In coordinates with this request, I have experienced biases and slurs with basic procedural matters when entering and exiting the District Court, filling court documents, and received mail documents. The same tactics that were used in District Court has taken place within this Circuit Court. When questioned a couple of the employees about the tactics there were discrepancies between their responses. Privacy door was closed when dealing with provided documents and awaiting a copy of the documents. Also, during this time a staff member stated that my case will not be heard in court anyway; meaning that there is a predetermined judgement within this case causing concerns of prejudices. These incidents took place on both dates of October 13, 2023 and October 20, 2023. Additionally, it is noted of the Judge's affiliation with the U.S. army, to which I have

activities, i.e previous acts as the States Attorne
of the local State police, County police, and Tow
for the service(s) that were and are of good faith.

Anticipated by,

been harassed locally by this respected group and this informat
have been publicly to the local community prior to this court cas
being forwarded to the Circuit Court.

2 of 3
L. Ce

At a previous position, I have been harassed by a Police Communications Office[redacted], that used to work with the Town of Princess Anne Police Department with the tactics of using staples and paper clips. These incidents have been and continues to be reported. This same tactic continues to be used within this local town even after the reports of this incident and is being used by the staffs of both District and Circuit Court and their affiliates.

As a previous States Attorney, it is known that there is a strong bond that Judge Daniel W. Powell has with the local policemen. With reviewing a couple of cases alone, shows the biases and connections of Judge Powell affiliations with the local police. For example, a case in 2015 as cas[redacted]hat included the statements of Princess Anne Police Dep[redacted]t to assist with the sentencing of [redacted]. All cases that I have reviewed just by randomly selecting a page and case within the Maryland Judiciary case search (page 15, bottom to top) shows that all cases were successful when [redacted]acted as a States Attorney (with the assistance of police) against civilians. The view of this and other cases are on the basis of the relationship that Judge Daniel Powell has with the local Town of Princess Anne Police; not the justice of jailing those that break the law. This brings about many conflict of interest concerns.

I respectfully ask you to recuse yourself from all Circuit Court proceedings where a potential conflict of interest exists or appea
exist between the possible outcomes of the case. Your pol

CIRCUIT COURT FOR SOMERSET COUNTY, MARYLAND

30512 Prince William Street
Princess Anne, Maryland 21853

Main: 410-845-4840
Fax: 410-845-4847

IN THE MATTER OF LA'ASIA CESAR

Case Number:
Tracking Number:
Related Case Number:

C-19-JV

NOTICE OF HEARING/TRIAL

Issue Date:

Please be advised that the following events have been scheduled in this case:

Date	Time	Type of Proceeding
04/19/2024	09:30AM	Hearing - Adjudication

Remarks:

Any postponement request must be filed in accordance with MD Rule 2-508 and addressed to the court address above.

Attorneys/parties shall notify this court immediately when a case settles before a scheduled event.

cc: La'asia Cesar
Somerset County Board Of Education
State's Attorney-Somerset County

---

impartially rule in these types of cases.

Currently, this case has been put into place to further violate many of my Amendment rights, stalk, harass and intimidate me. This case is where the Landing/Webster family were included in session. Since the date I found out that this family was included in the harassment. Only to be made known that Somerset County Public Schools have been notified of my child not attending the public school system way back in August 2023.

The matter is that your personal interests may conflict with the interests of being able to provide the proper service and release of transcripts. Especially since the cost(s) you provided seems to be for 1 transcript (and is incorrect). Whereas, I requested 2 transcripts and the costs for each are $25 per transcript; totaling $50. It is unknown for the reason you would be in charge of transcripts for another county. Which leads to more of a reason and evident of the matter being covered up leading to corruption within the local judicial system. You all will need to kill me to stop me from speaking up. I will not be silenced until that day.

A civilian with integrity,
La'Asia Cesar

IN THE MATTER OF CASE NO. C-19-JV-23-000057

IN THE CIRCUIT COURT FOR

LA'ASIA CESAR   SOMERSET COUNTY, MARYLAND

SITTING AS JUVENILE COURT

To the State of Maryland, Somerset County, to wit:

To the Sheriff of Somerset County, Greeting:

You are hereby commanded to subpoena the below named person if found in your County, to appear before **CIRCUIT COURT FOR SOMERSET COUNTY, 30512 PRINCE WILLIAM ST., PRINCESS ANNE, MD 21853** at 9:00 AM, on **Friday, February 16, 2024**, to testify in the above-captioned proceedings.

In Maryland Circuit Court for Somerset County
State of Maryland vs La'Asia Cesar

C19JV23000057

Defendant
La'Asia Cesar

3/25/2024

Plaintiff
Somerset County Circuit Court
Truancy Court
30512 Princess William Street
Princess Anne, MD 21853

Re: Motion for Trial by Jury

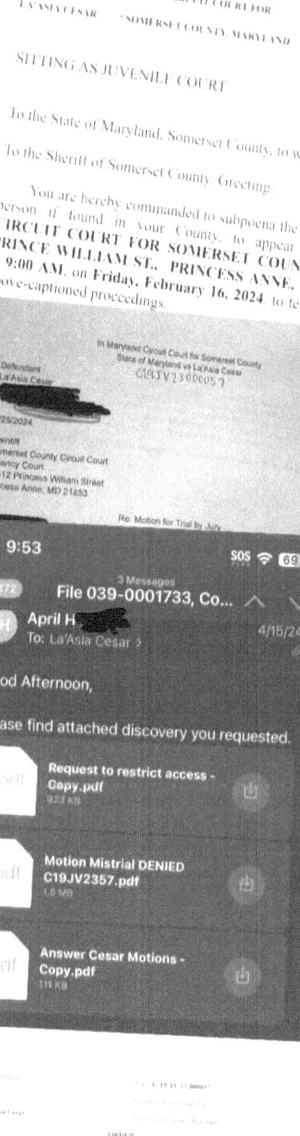

Somerset County, Maryland

STATE'S ANSWER TO RESPONDENT'S MOTIONS

The State, Kristen Boston, Assistant State's Attorney for Somerset County, Maryland, Respondent's Motions for a Witness List, Motion to Shield, Motion to Make Case and Motion for Mistrial and in support thereof states, to wit:

1. As to Respondent's Motion for a Witness List, the State notes that it intends to call Charti Jones, 7982-A Lowes Campus Drive, Westover, MD 21871 as a witness.

2. As to Respondent's Motion to Shield, the State notes that as this case is file under the juvenile jurisdiction the matter is confidential, thereby protecting the identity of the child at issue.

3. As to Respondent's Motion to Make the Case Public, the State notes that opening this proceeding goes against the intent of their Motion to Shield.

4. As to Respondent's Motion to Dismiss, or Motion for Mistrial, the State notes that there is no issue with the child in this case receiving a private or homeschool education, the only matter at issue is ensuring that Respondent fills out the appropriate paperwork and complies with the procedures required to ensure that the child is receiving education in all core areas. This compliance must conform to the same standards and norms as required of all parents. The State has no malice for anyone involved in this case, and only seeks to ensure compliance with the laws as they relate to this case. A mistrial, or dismissal, is inappropriate at this time.

WHEREFORE, the State requests the Court

ORDER

IT IS ORDERED
DENIED / DISMISSED

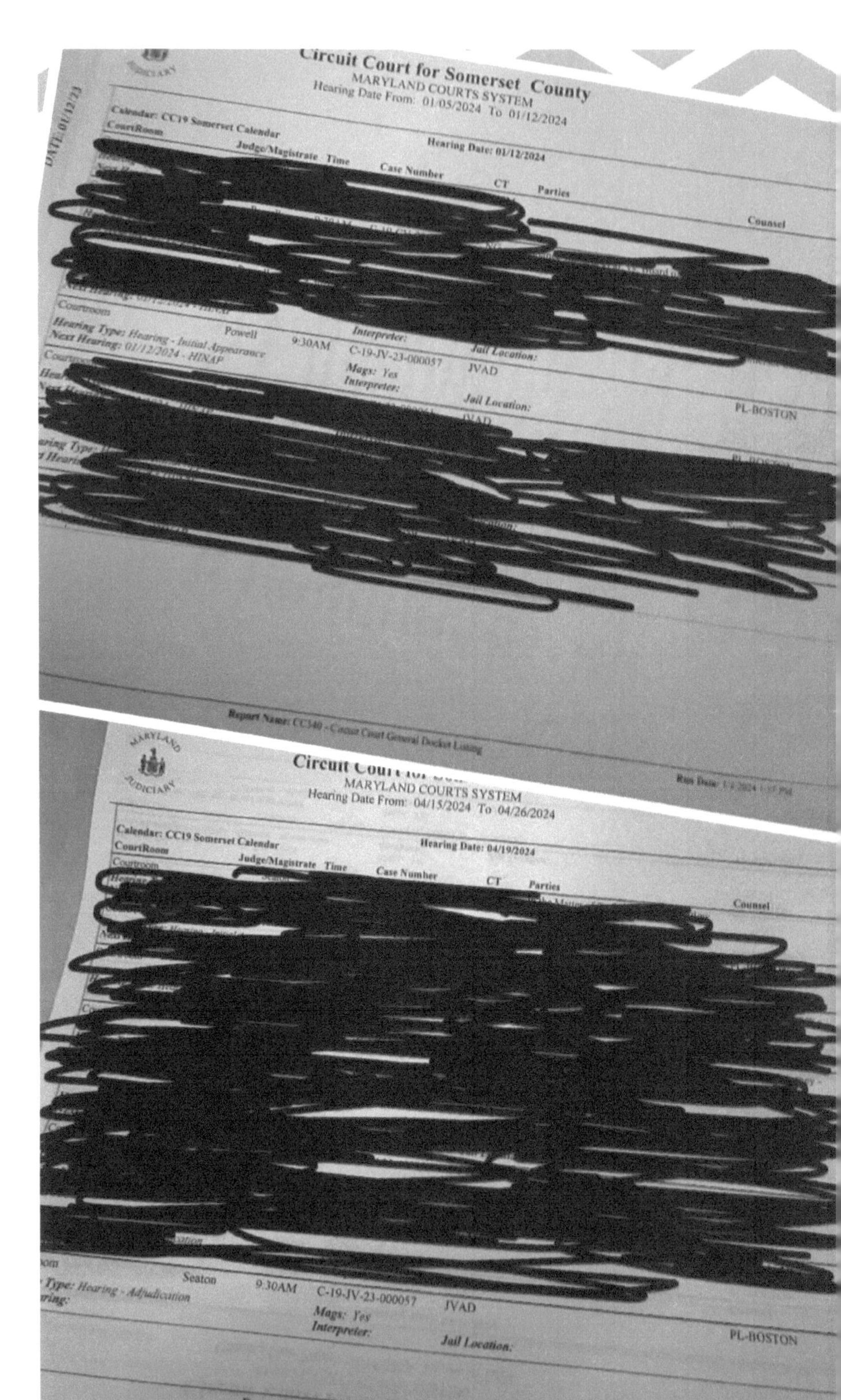

Circuit Court for Somerset County
MARYLAND COURTS SYSTEM
Hearing Date From: 01/05/2024 To 01/12/2024

Calendar: CC19 Somerset Calendar

CourtRoom

Hearing Date: 01/12/2024

Judge/Magistrate	Time	Case Number	CT	Parties	Counsel

Courtroom

Hearing Type: Hearing - Initial Appearance Powell 9:30AM C-19-JV-23-000057 JVAD
Next Hearing: 01/12/2024 - HINAP

Interpreter:

Jail Location:

Mags: Yes

Interpreter:

Jail Location: JVAD PL-BOSTON

Circuit Court for Somerset County
MARYLAND COURTS SYSTEM
Hearing Date From: 04/15/2024 To 04/26/2024

Run Date: 1/4/2024 1:07 PM

Calendar: CC19 Somerset Calendar

CourtRoom

Hearing Date: 04/19/2024

Judge/Magistrate	Time	Case Number	CT	Parties	Counsel

Type: Hearing - Adjudication Seaton 9:30AM C-19-JV-23-000057 JVAD
ring:

Mags: Yes

Interpreter:

Jail Location: PL-BOSTON

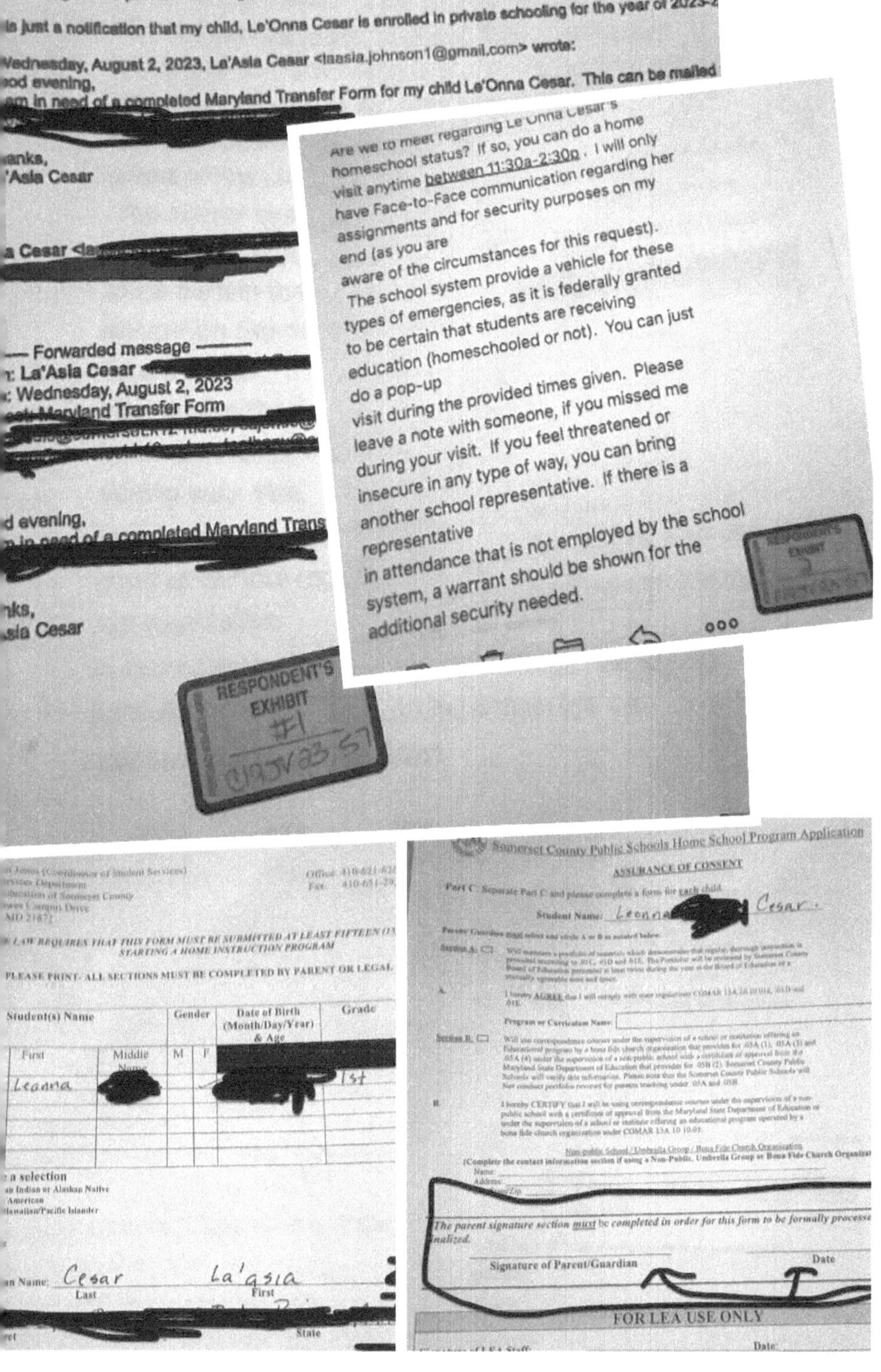

is just a notification that my child, Le'Onna Cesar is enrolled in private schooling for the year of 2023-2

Wednesday, August 2, 2023, La'Asia Cesar <laasia.johnson1@gmail.com> wrote:
od evening,
m in need of a completed Maryland Transfer Form for my child Le'Onna Cesar. This can be mailed

anks,
'Asia Cesar

a Cesar <la

—— Forwarded message ———
: La'Asia Cesar <
: Wednesday, August 2, 2023
t: Maryland Transfer Form

d evening,
n in need of a completed Maryland Trans

nks,
sia Cesar

Are we to meet regarding Le'Onna Cesar's homeschool status? If so, you can do a home visit anytime between 11:30a-2:30p. I will only have Face-to-Face communication regarding her assignments and for security purposes on my end (as you are aware of the circumstances for this request). The school system provide a vehicle for these types of emergencies, as it is federally granted to be certain that students are receiving education (homeschooled or not). You can just do a pop-up visit during the provided times given. Please leave a note with someone, if you missed me during your visit. If you feel threatened or insecure in any type of way, you can bring another school representative. If there is a representative in attendance that is not employed by the school system, a warrant should be shown for the additional security needed.

Somerset County Public Schools Home School Program Application

ASSURANCE OF CONSENT

Part C: Separate Part C and please complete a form for each child.

Student Name: Leonna ███ Cesar

Parent/Guardian must select and circle A or B as noted below.

Section A: Will maintain a portfolio of materials which demonstrate that regular, thorough instruction is provided according to .01C, .01D and .01E. The Portfolio will be reviewed by Somerset County Board of Education personnel at least twice during the year at the Board of Education in a mutually agreeable time and space.

A. I hereby AGREE that I will comply with state regulations COMAR 13A.10.01.01A, .01D and .01E.

Program or Curriculum Name: ____________

Section B: Will use correspondence course under the supervision of a school or institution offering an Educational program by a bona fide church organization that provides for .05A (1), .05A (3) and .05A (4) under the supervision of a non-public school with a certificate of approval from the Maryland State Department of Education that provides for .05B (2). Somerset County Public Schools will verify this information. Please note that the Somerset County Public Schools will Not conduct portfolio reviews for parents teaching under .05A and .05B.

B. I hereby CERTIFY that I will be using correspondence courses under the supervision of a non-public school with a certificate of approval from the Maryland State Department of Education or under the supervision of a school or institute offering an educational program operated by a bona fide church organization under COMAR 13A.10.05.

Non-public School / Umbrella Group / Bona Fide Church Organization
(Complete the contact information section if using a Non-Public, Umbrella Group or Bona Fide Church Organization)
Name: ____________
Address: ____________
City/State/Zip: ____________

The parent signature section must be completed in order for this form to be formally processed/finalized.

Signature of Parent/Guardian: ____________   Date: ____________

FOR LEA USE ONLY

Signature of LEA Staff: ____________   Date: ____________

Jones (Coordinator of Student Services)   Office: 410-621-62
rvices Department   Fax: 410-651-29
lucation of Somerset County
ves Campus Drive
MD 21871

LAW REQUIRES THAT THIS FORM MUST BE SUBMITTED AT LEAST FIFTEEN D
STARTING A HOME INSTRUCTION PROGRAM

PLEASE PRINT- ALL SECTIONS MUST BE COMPLETED BY PARENT OR LEGAL

Student(s) Name		Gender		Date of Birth (Month/Day/Year) & Age	Grade
First	Middle Nam	M	F		
Leaana					1st

a selection
an Indian or Alaskan Native
American
Hawaiian/Pacific Islander

an Name: Cesar   La'asia
          Last   First

Verification of Enrollment

August 1, 2023

To whom it may concern,

This letter is to certify that the following student is enrolled in ███████████ for the 2023-2024 school year and is in full compliance with the compulsory attendance laws of the state.

Student Name	Date of Birth	Enrollment Period
Cesar Le'Onna	███████	8/1/2023 - 7/31/2024

If you have any additional questions, please do not hesitate to contact me.

Kind regards,

███████ Academy

Your Story

Reflections

Please reflect on your thoughts regarding the case. Was it a retaliatory incident? Please keep our me in your prayers as I continue to navigate these challenges within our community. If you find yourself in a similar situation, take note of your thoughts and turn to prayer for guidance. Thank you for taking the time to read about my family's journey.

About the Author

La'Asia Cesar is a woman of courage, resilience, and unwavering faith. Her journey through a legal battle, marked by trials and tribulations, is a testament to her unyielding spirit and steadfast belief in justice.

Born with a passion for giving back to her community, La'Asia embarked on a journey of education and self-improvement. She earned her degree in Chemical Dependency from Wor-Wic Community College, and later pursued a degree in Conflict Analysis and Dispute Resolution with a minor in Psychology at Salisbury University. Her pursuit of knowledge didn't stop there; she went on to pursue a dual Master's Degree in Applied Family Science and Case Management Certification from Wilmington University. Despite facing adversity at Wilmington University, including a suspension due to circumstances beyond her control, she remained resolute in her pursuit of her goals of wanting to guide others.

Despite her academic achievements, La'Asia found herself engulfed in a retaliatory legal battle that would test her resolve like never before. As she stood before the judge, ready to present her case, she was met with pressure from the state's attorney to settle by signing a homeschooling document. However, La'Asia remained resolute, refusing to compromise her rights and her child's education.

Representing herself in court, La'Asia faced numerous challenges and obstacles. Despite moments of doubt and fear, she persevered, guided by her unwavering faith in God's plan. As the legal proceedings unfolded, La'Asia's faith was put to the ultimate test, as she faced the prospect of jail time for standing up for what she believed in.

In the face of adversity, La'Asia remained steadfast, drawing strength from her faith and the support of her family. Her refusal to back down in the face of injustice ultimately led to divine intervention, as the states attorney and judge swiftly dismissed the case, recognizing the righteousness of her cause.